VOLCANOES

WHY DO THEY HAPPEN?

Speedy Publishing LLC
40 E. Main St. #1156
Newark, DE 19711
www.speedypublishing.com

Copyright 2018

All Rights reserved. No part of this book may be reproduced or used in any way or form or by any means whether electronic or mechanical, this means that you cannot record or photocopy any material ideas or tips that are provided in this book.

A volcano is a rupture on the crust
of a planetary-mass object, such as
Earth, that allows hot lava, volcanic
ash, and gases to escape from a
magma chamber below the surface.

Volcanoes are just a natural way that the Earth and other planets have of cooling off and releasing internal heat and pressure.

A volcano can be active, dormant or extinct state. An active volcano is one that erupts regularly. A dormant volcano is one that has not erupted for many years, although there is still some activity deep inside. an extinct volcano is one that has been dormant for over 2,000 years and has not shown any sign if activity.

Volcanoes are formed when magma from within the Earth's upper mantle works its way to the surface. At the surface, it erupts to form lava flows and ash deposits.

Over time as the volcano continues to erupt, it will get bigger and bigger.

Volcanoes grow by intrusion and extrusion.

An intrusion is magma that moves up into a volcano without erupting.

An extrusion is an
eruption of material
that causes the
volcano to grow on
the outside.

Eruptions can occur without any preceding signals, making them extremely difficult to predict. Sometimes there are useful clues for judging when a volcano is likely to erupt. A volcano's history may provide some clues.

Volcanoes erupt because
of the gas trapped inside
magma, not the magma itself,
ultimately forces an eruption.
The types of gases include
water vapor, carbon dioxide,
sulfur dioxide, hydrogen
sulfide, hydrogen chloride,
and other very strong acids.

Magma deep in the mantle
is under a lot of pressure,
and so its gases stay
dissolved in the liquid. It
will rise to the surface or to
a depth that is determined
by the density of the
magma and the weight of
the rocks above it.

Bubbles start to form from the gas dissolved in the magma. The gas bubbles exert tremendous pressure. This pressure helps to bring the magma to the surface and forces it in the air, sometimes to great heights.

Magma reaching the surface of the earth is referred as lava. Over the period of time through constant eruption, layer by layer of lava builds up a volcano.

Lava cools slowly because lava is a poor conductor of heat. Lava flows slow down and thicken as they harden.

Volcanic
eruptions can
send ash high
into the air,
over 30km (17
miles) above
the Earth's
surface.

www.ingramcontent.com/pod-product-compliance
Lightning Source LLC
Chambersburg PA
CBHW080251180726
47999CB00019B/2815